MY ~~BOOK~~

OVERSEAS

AUGUST 21st 1944 till OCTOBER 8th 1946

INDIA - SEPTEMBER 21st 1944 till DECEMBER 31st 1944

BURMA - JANUARY 1945 till NOVEMBER 1945

MALAYA - DECEMBER 1945 till SEPTEMBER 1946

By

N. A. SHINFIELD

(Royal Air Force)

Edited by
Robert Shinfield

Grosvenor House
Publishing Limited

This book is published by
Grosvenor House Publishing Ltd
Link House
140 The Broadway, Tolworth, Surrey, KT6 7HT.
www.grosvenorhousepublishing.co.uk

A CIP record for this book
is available from the British Library

ISBN 978-1-80381-890-0

CONTENTS

FOREWORD

Noel Albert Shinfield was born in Braintree, Essex on 19th December 1924. He died from COVID, after a lengthy fight against dementia, on 20th May 2020. A few months after his death, my sister and I set about sorting through the memorabilia of his life, much of it boxed up at the bottom of a wardrobe. Amongst photo albums, postcards, letters and various pieces of paperwork we found this diary.

We already knew that dad joined the RAF in 1943 at the age of 18. We also knew that he travelled with them to India and Burma as a radio technician. But that was about all. He never really spoke to us about his years at war. And we never asked him to.

So on first reading, the contents of this diary were as new to us then as they will be to you now.

It is no great work of prose, true. But it does represent an authentic account of a young man travelling to war, his thoughts, feelings and fears.

As stated in the contents page - the original account has been edited a little by myself. This was wholly for the purposes of correcting spelling and grammar, weeding out unnecessary repetition and making sure that all events flow chronologically. Otherwise, it is the true and full voice of the author.

For accuracy, I have researched spellings of place names and corrected where possible. I have also researched acronyms. However, despite my best efforts, some spellings and acronyms have remained untraceable, so apologies if any of these are misspelt or inaccurate.

Dad, I hope you are proud of what has been achieved here.

ROBERT SHINFIELD

CHAPTER I

CONCERNING THE VOYAGE

It was on a glorious summer's evening late in August, the 24th to be exact, that our troopship SS Otranto sailed slowly down the Clyde towards the open sea and then onwards to where? We didn't know!

The day this story begins was one of great sadness for the majority of us, for on that fateful day we saw the last of our beloved country Britain for many years to come.

The boat onto which we were packed was a 22,000 ton ship of the 'Orient Line.' She had been built in 1925, and many of us thought she should have been destroyed many years ago. However, it was this ship, which incidentally was called the "Attmark," which was to be our home for the next 28 days.

As we sailed past the boon just beyond Greenock, we saw the last of Scotland's variously hued mountains in the gathering dusk. My last impression of Blighty on that evening, as I cast my eyes upon those gorgeous arrays of colour, was that I would never find a better or more beautiful land wherever I travelled.

As it soon got dark, and we were all required below deck, we left that final scene to be impressed on our memories for a long time to come. I often wondered what it would be like to leave England, and now I knew. It was a very peculiar and depressing feeling.

When we got below to our mess deck, which, us only being common airmen, was just on the water line, we were given all the rules and regulations of the ship. We were then given our hammocks and other items which we would require on board ship.

After what had been a rather exhausting day, we were all very glad to get below and into our hammocks. If anyone thought he was going to get a comfortable night's rest though, for his first night on board ship, he was hopelessly wrong. Getting settled in a hammock is a thing which would take quite a bit of getting used to, for you were always in constant dread of falling out. When you did get so called comfy, the heat below deck caused by lack of fresh air, and many other things adhering to the working of a ship, was sometimes unbearable and suffocating.

The next day we were all up very early to see where we were or what was in sight, but to our great disappointment all we could see was a slightly rough sea, and in the far distance on our port side, what we were told was Ireland.

As we sailed on through the day, going due west all the time, we zig-zagged, just in case we went into any submarine packs. The day which had started fine was now getting dull with a fairly heavy sea, indicating the approach of bad weather.

During the next few days, we were soon to find out we weren't far from wrong, for the ship rolled and pitched to the fury of a storm swept sea. Of course by now, many of the troops were feeling the ill effects of the ever rolling sea. To make things worse, it was too warm to stay below deck and too cold upon deck so we had to bear one or the other. I myself chose on deck for there was a certain amount of interest up there.

The main interest on deck was watching the other ships of our large convoy. There were six troopships in all, with an escort of several destroyers and aircraft carriers. The six ships were all carrying troops bound for different parts of the world. One ship, which we soon found out was our sister ship 'Orantis,' was bound for Italy, whilst another was heading for Egypt. The other three ships and ourselves were bound for India.

On our third day out, we veered towards the south. We felt that we must have been halfway to the U.S.A. before this change of course. In fact, we had all had hopes of going to Canada, although at the time the main rumour was Algeria. Now our course had changed, the weather certainly improved and there was only a slight roll on the ship.

We sailed in this direction for little longer than a day and were soon heading east, which as we more or less guessed meant the Mediterranean Sea. On the fifth day, before we were due to enter the Mediterranean by passing our fortress at Gibraltar, the sea suddenly calmed down, in fact many of us believed we were already in the Mediterranean.

We passed Gibraltar in the dead of night, so very few of us saw it. Those who did, either guards or men otherwise employed, said they saw the lights of Morocco. After the blackouts back home, they were the first lights they had seen for many years.

We had now been sailing for a week and had all survived the journey very well so far. Except for the usual cases of sea sickness which 80% of the troops went down with, there was very little other illness on board. Now the sea had calmed down and was in fact reasonably smooth, we were all feeling much better. Of course, the weather had also greatly improved and it was getting so much warmer. We could now laze on the deck and bask in the sun, for the sky was almost cloudless for the many days of our sail through this great inland sea. We also found out that the sea lived up to its beautiful blue reputation.

Perhaps at this point of the narrative I should describe to you something of the life on board ship, where one more or less followed the rules of the ship's crew. The day started by getting up at 6:00am followed by breakfast which mostly consisted of porridge, bacon or sausage, bread, butter & jam and coffee. After this meal, there was a thorough clean up of our mess-deck in preparation for the ship's captain's inspection. This was carried out by 10:00am whilst we were all massed at boat stations during boat drill. After this, unless unlucky to be picked for fatigues, we were free for the rest of the day.

Tiffin was served at midday and supper, the last meal of the day, at 6:00pm. In the evenings it was best and often coolest to go up on deck, where they often had singing led by the padre.

Of course there was very little to do on board except sit and chat or play some games. I myself often used to play chess with one of my mates, Bob, who came from Manchester. In the evenings, three of us; Bob, Ray (a fellow from Sussex) and myself used to have discussions on any subject that was going. It was surprising what topics did occur in our quiet evening chats - anything from war positions, which at that time were good, to railway engines.

To get back to the story, we slowly sailed on through the Mediterranean Sea at an average speed of 18 knots. On the third day, we passed some land which we found out to be Pantelleria, an island we had captured off the Italians earlier on in the war. The sighting of land caused a great amount of excitement as it was the first we had seen for over a week. I am sure we caused a list to the port side of our ship. Anyway, this brief glimpse of land was soon over and we were once more miles from anywhere. It was on this same day that our sister ship left us for Italy.

Two days later, we once again saw land, but this time it was Egypt and we followed its coastline for that day.

Later on in the day, we saw Alexandria in the distance, although we weren't near enough to see anything of interest.

In the morning we all rushed on deck to see our first sight of life since leaving Blighty a fortnight previously. What met our eyes on that morning was a city with many large buildings standing at the entrance of the Suez Canal and, under the guidance of many fussing little ships we made our way into Port Said.

We were tied up there for a day whilst refuelling and awaiting our turn to pass down the Suez. Whilst here, we were pestered by many Arabs rowing out in their small boats trying to sell us everything under the sun. When the evening came, to our great surprise, the city was all lit up, the first time we had seen this for five years. It was a wonderful sight to behold and we spent several hours wandering around the ship, taking in the lights of the city which practically surrounded us. It was up to the present the most interesting day we had spent, although the next day was to be far more so, as we were about to find out.

Early the next day we started our journey down the great Suez Canal, which streaks across the desert for 100 miles. On both sides of us stretched miles of sandy plains. On our port side ran a railway; a single track affair which ran from Port Suez to Port Said. The banks of the canal were very close to the ship, in fact once we did hit the side with a resounding bang. In the afternoon we entered the first of the great salt lakes, which form part of the canal. At the beginning of the lake there was the lovely little township of Ismalia, where there was a Royal Air Force station.

After passing through the two lakes we continued along the last few miles of the canal and then out into the Gulf of Suez. All through this canal, it had been very funny to look back and see what looked like a ship going through the desert. Of course we were being ridiculed, as all forces are, by other forces on the bank, who kept on shouting; "You're going the wrong way chum." And we were!!

The heat was now getting stifling and we were finding it very oppressive indeed. We had now got permission to sleep on deck where it was very much cooler and we were all able to sleep much better. We spent three days at Port Suez where we had our only film show. We stood a little too far off from the land to see very much of interest, so it got very monotonous and we were very glad to get out to sea again.

As we sailed down the Red Sea, which lives up to its namesake, it began to get very hot. In fact the temperature was often above 110°F. There was very little breeze and what breeze there was, was hot as it had just crossed the Arabian Desert. It was during this part of the journey that most of the illness occurred on board due to the heat that none of us were used to. We were all glad to see Aden where, although it was still hot, there was a much cooler breeze blowing.

Aden, one of Britain's most outlandish pieces of the Empire, stands on a rocky plain stretching out to sea with a range of mountains behind it, making it look very formidable to anyone who may wish to attack it. There were many large and modern buildings, which was in great contrast to the native town behind. However, we only stayed for one day so were not able to get a very good impression of it.

The following morning, we were off again out into the Arabian Sea and the last leg of our journey. The sea was once more a vivid blue, a nice change after the Red Sea. It also seemed very much cooler, for now there was a cool breeze blowing.

At last! India was reached after sailing steadily for five days across the Arabian Sea. We approached it from the west, first vaguely seeing it in the distance in the early morning. Our first impression of the great city of Bombay was that it was a very modern city, much like a British city.

We stood off it, in the bay for a day and then went into the docks where they started to unload our kit.

CHAPTER II

INDIA – LAND OF SMELLS

On the morning of 20th September, we were all massed on deck in full marching order prior to disembarking. We got our orders to move very soon and were off the ship on to land once again. We were then loaded into gharries (lorries) and away to our new camp.

Our reception camp was about 4 miles outside Bombay. It was built on the side of a hill coming down to the sea front, from where we could see Bombay. On our journey to the camp we did not see much of Bombay so did not get much of an impression first time.

When we arrived at the camp, we were given billets, which were built of brick and housed about a hundred men each. We then went through the usual business of lectures and getting booked into camp. We soon found out that the food at this camp was to be very much better than we had been eating on board ship, so we soon got our appetites back to normal.

Of course, for the first few days, we found ourselves drinking as much as possible for you needed to keep up with all you were losing due to sweating. We had a canteen on the camp where we could always get a cold drink, so we never had to go thirsty.

That first night in Worli was one which would stick in my mind for many years to come. We were careful to obey all anti-malaria precautions by getting our nets down at least two hours before darkness, just in case any mosquitoes decided to come out a little earlier than usual.

When it came to time to go to bed, everyone very quickly nipped in under their nets, expecting at least a hundred mosquitoes to follow them in. Needless to say, this was not the case. Once we were in bed, we inspected it for anything we might find - like snakes. By the time you had carried out all of this, the bed was in such a mess, you just lay on top of it exhausted.

The next day we were off down into Bombay to have a real look at the place. We left the camp and soon found ourselves pestered by many locals trying to sell us anything, especially fruit. However, fruit being one of the worst causes of diseases in this country, we left it well alone, unless bought off official fruit wallahs! We were able to get oranges, limes, bananas and many other delicious fruits we had not seen for many years.

My first impression of Bombay was one of a large and modern city with wide roads. Mixed into this were the native houses, horse drawn vehicles and bullock carts, whose drivers were nearly always asleep.

The worst thing about the place was the terrible and putrid smells which, in due time we got used to, like most things in India.

We were only to stay in Bombay for a week and so, with these mixed and varying thoughts of a new country, we left Worli for the station. It was during this short journey that I got the most awful views of India. People were sleeping everywhere; on the pavements, in the gutters, in fact in every conceivable place you could think of. I was therefore very relieved when we got on the 4:00am train and left for Poona.

A wonderful sight met our eyes when we awoke, for we were wending our way through the mountains with a sheer drop on one side and soaring cliffs on the other. We finally travelled on to the plain upon which stands Poona.

Perhaps here I should mention the luxurious Indian trains. We, of course, travelled third class which basically consisted of hard wooden benches. They were also infested with cockroaches, as big as half-crowns, running over you as you slept. The speed of these trains never exceeds 25mph, unless you are lucky enough to get an express which is not very often. I think that, of all the modes of transport I have travelled in, this was undoubtedly the worst.

We arrived in Poona that afternoon, but were soon in another train heading for Belgaum. This time we were lucky enough to procure a first class carriage and enjoyed

11

a very pleasant journey indeed. There were fans and showers, in fact every convenience possible. As the evening drew on, we slowly puffed our way up into the Gats (Ghats), climbing all the while till we were 6,000 feet above sea level. The turns and gradients that railway took seemed impossible for any train to overcome.

The following morning, we found ourselves pulled into Belgaum. There we managed to get a cup of tea from some WVS. We ere then loaded into gharries, and after a rough and dusty ride, we arrived at our new camp of Sambre!

The camp, which consisted of billets and tents, was situated in the middle of a village - not a very hygienic place for a camp. We had the misfortune to be stuck in tents, which we did not particularly fancy, as the monsoon was still not quite over. Our first impressions of Sambre were not what we would call good, for tented life was not all that exciting. Besides being a training camp, there was also a lot of unwanted discipline, which the lads didn't take to much. We thought we had left all that behind in Blighty, but in the next two months we found we were very wrong.

Sambre, which is a small village, lays about 60 miles east of Portuguese Goa up in the Western Ghats. It is very nicely situated and has a nice climate - not too hot or cold. It stands on a plain surrounded by very high hills.

On the camp itself there was a decent cinema and also occasionally we got an ENSA show. Later on, after we had left, they built a swimming pool. So, as for entertainment, we were really not able to grumble, for we had all we wanted.

For the first week at camp, we did nothing but drill, physical training and once we went driving. We all used to look forward so much to these driving classes, for they broke the monotony of the other training. This training, we were told, was to get us fit and ready for forward areas where most of us were bound for.

It was after this first week of training that I was taken ill with a slight attack of malaria. I was soon taken away to a military hospital in Belgaum, where I was kept for over a week. It was such a lovely change here, for we were looked after by British nurses and we got the best of attention. Anyhow, the time soon flew by and I was discharged and back to more training.

Just after I came out of hospital, we were all medically examined and placed into different categories. "Assault" was the highest and meant anyone in that category was fit for any service in the Royal Air Force. "Mobile," to which I belonged, wasn't quite so strenuous.

We now began our real training, going on long route marches and often being out all day long. One particular day's marching sticks out in my memory more than any other. We set out at 8:00am intending to cross over a range of hills and return by the road. After we had been marching for several hours, we found ourselves lost. And the only way out was through some paddy fields.

On and on we waded, knee deep, often neck deep through the waterlogged ground. We must have waded for 5 or 6 hours before we finally struck the road and were picked up by gharries. When we got back at 7:00pm, they decided to allow us to parade a whole half an hour later the next morning. It must have broken their hearts to be so lenient with us.

A few days later, we were off on another scheme, this time a jungle penetration, which consisted of cutting our way through uncharted forests and crossing flooded rivers. Having done all of these things, we were now drawing towards the end of our course.

A few days later, our postings came through. Also I got put on my first charge. I was stopped by an officer after dark for not having my sleeves rolled down. The next day I was brought before the CO and was awarded 4 days CC. It was the last day of my punishment that we had our final check up and were told we were going to Calcutta for further postings. It was on this day that I joined 5837 Mobile Signals Unit.

The unit, at that moment, consisted of four men and one corporal. The four men were: Jimmy from Manchester - a Radio Telegraph Operator, Stanley from London - a motor mechanic, Johnny from Bristol and myself - both Wireless Mechanics.

It was upon joining this unit that I left Sambre and also my best pal, Bob. It seemed quite hard to say goodbye to him for we had been together for over 6 months.

So on the 15th November we left Sambre, bound for the station and a journey which was to bring us many happy and exciting adventures during the next year.

We arrived at Belgaum station at 6:00pm, but as usual were kept hanging around. Belgaum itself is only a small town but surprisingly clean for India. At midnight, we boarded the train again, travelling third class. Once again we were on the Poona line, although this time we were heading in the opposite direction. We arrived at Poona early the next afternoon where we changed trains. The train we got into was more or less habitable for our four days journey. It had a dining car attached where all our food was prepared and cooked. We left Poona at about midnight and, when we awoke, found ourselves at a fair sized town called Igatpuri, where we had our breakfast on the platform.

We soon left and were steaming across the hot and flat plains, with nothing but scrub all around us. It was during this journey that I began to see life more or less in its true surroundings. We passed many straggling villages which mostly consisted of a few bamboo huts built around a dirty swamp. The children would run along beside the train shouting; "Rupees Sahib," which meant they wanted money. At first we threw out odd coins but that soon had to be stopped, lest we would have been broke, for there were thousands of them.

The following morning saw us in Nagpur, which is in the central provinces. It was a very large town but, of course, as in all Indian towns, the poverty showed up everywhere.

We couldn't see much of the town for we were not allowed off the train, but what we could see of it looked quite modern.

When we left Nagpur mid-morning, we started to wend our way once again through the hills. We climbed and dropped all day long. In fact, as every station had its elevation below its name, we used to guess how high we were. Finally, in the evening, as it began to get dark, we pulled out onto the long plain once again.

In the morning, when we awoke we found ourselves at Hingin, still in the central provinces. We had our breakfast here and were soon away again across the flat and uninteresting country. The thing that seemed so funny to me was that so little of it was cultivated.

We were all very glad to see Calcutta the next morning and were soon taken to our transit camp. That evening, Henderson, a pal from Coventry, and I set out to have a look at Calcutta but were greatly disappointed for it was all blacked out. What little we could see was that it was a large town with all modern conveniences. The main street, Chowringhee was long with one side bordered by shops and cinemas and the other side parklands. It was here we first met with the rickshaw, a hand driven vehicle which carries one or two persons.

There were few decent cinemas in Calcutta. One which was called the "Lighthouse," was the best cinema I have ever been in. Instead of the seats sloping down towards the screen, they slope upwards so you can lay back and enjoy the film.

The next day, we were split into three parties; one for Comilla, one for Chittagong and one for Imphal! It seemed to us then that they could hardly send fellows like us to Imphal where all the fighting had been. But they did, and there is no denying it, I had a sinking feeling inside me.

The other two parties left and we were due to depart on Saturday. We got down to the station with all of our kit following us behind but, as usual, due to all the muddle, our kit arrived late - half an hour after the train had gone! So back we went to camp for three more days.

The night before we did finally leave Calcutta, three of us celebrated something or other and had a really wizard meal at "Furpas." Although it cost us quite a fair amount, we had a really good feed so we could not grumble and were perfectly happy and contented when we had finished.

The train left with us all on board the following afternoon and we were once more being dashed across the countryside of India. This was most likely to be our last view of India, so we took it all in with great interest. Early in the evening, we crossed the Ganges by one of the most amazing bits of engineering I have ever seen. It was a bridge with 19 spans, which must have been nearly a mile long.

Late that evening, we once again changed trains and were soon travelling all through the night. At about

11:00am we arrived at a station where we were all told to get out and straggled down to a wharf. From here we were to catch a ferry across the Brahmaputra; India's eastern frontier, a dark brown swirling river, easily two miles across. On the other side lay Manipur State, Burma!

This great natural river barrier may have played a big part in the war if the Japs had ever reached it, which of course thanks to our English Johnny, they didn't.

As the ferry started to slowly cross, many weird thoughts flew through our minds of what was in store for us on the other side.

CHAPTER III

Across the Brahmaputra

As soon as we reached the other side, we were rushed upon by hundreds of coolies to help carry our kit to the awaiting train, which was to take us to Dinapur, our next stop on the journey. After walking for about half a mile, we reached the train, thinking ourselves lucky we had not had to carry our kit, which we dumped on the platform before making off for a transit camp where we were to eat. We all enjoyed the meal very much, for it was the first we'd had since the previous evening. After we had all eaten, we had a shower, a wash and then back to the train.

The train left at 4:00pm and we were soon puffing our way up through the hills, another natural barrier. We travelled all night through these hills and when we awoke, found ourselves in Dinapur. There, we were told to all get out and were soon loaded into gharries. We now started our 125 mile journey along the Manipur road to Imphal. This journey was one of the most interesting I have ever made. We climbed steadily for hours, twisting and turning up the steep gradients. On one side of us there was a towering cliff, whilst on the other, a sheer drop of a thousand feet or more. We kept on climbing with less than 100 yards between each turn, sometimes finding ourselves going back the way we had come, only this time on the other side of the ravine. After travelling for about sixty miles, it began to get rather chilly and some of us were pulling on our greatcoats.

By now we had arrived at Kohima, the famous village where the 14th Army made their brilliant stand and later, advances. There was, of course, nothing left of it except for a few shattered ruins and shrubs.

We could now see why we had made such a determined stand there, for this road was the lifeline between India and Burma.

It was near here we stopped and had our dinner, which came in very welcome. After this meal, we continued along the twisting, climbing road until we reached the top at 10,000ft. By now, my ears were thumping and I had quite a headache, caused by the great height - higher than I'd ever been before.

Anyway, we were soon dropping at a much greater speed than we had climbed and we presently came upon an open plain which showed signs of where we were. There were tank depots, men resting and guns going forward so we guessed we were somewhere in the forward areas. After a few more miles, we passed an airstrip which we found out was Imphal strip. A mile or two further and we pulled up at an army rest camp, not that I could see anything restful about it.

We had long bamboo shelves to sleep on, three at a time. We were all very tired and soon got our beds down, making them just as usual with one sheet on top. To our great discomfort, in the middle of the night we awoke shivering with cold, even after putting on our greatcoats. In the morning, we dashed around trying to get ourselves warm and we were all very glad when the sun came out and helped to warm us through.

In the afternoon, we set out to find our unit which we were told was at Tallihul airstrip. When we got there, we could find no trace of it. But, as it was getting dark, we spent the night there, intending next day to find it.

The following day, we did indeed find our unit which was stationed at Number 9 Operations Room. We were first of all given Charpoys (beds) and a little billet to sleep in and were told to report next day. We were, of course, as always at any new station, anxious to see if there was any mail for us. And to our great delight we found there was.

This camp, to which we had taken a liking from the first moment, had billets built out of bamboo and straw called 'bashas.' It was very nicely laid out with footpaths everywhere and every convenience one could think of.

The climate here is well worth mentioning. It was in the beginning of December when we got there which, in this part of the world, is winter time. During the day it was lovely and warm, although not too warm, but at night it got so cold that you needed at least three blankets on you. We often used to get up in the morning and find ice on the food. All the same, it was a climate we enjoyed, for no matter how cold it was, you could always manage to keep warm.

When we reported for work next morning, we were shown around the place and found we were to work on VHF equipment.

We were soon settling down to our work and quite enjoying ourselves at Imphal. We were also getting plenty of time off. In fact we were working 24 hours every four days. In the town there was a YMCA where we could go when we came off duty. We also had a cinema, where the film changed twice a week.

It was now drawing forward to our first Christmas and none of us were looking forward much to our first one overseas. On the Saturday before Christmas, a few of us went to a carol service, where we had a very enjoyable evening indeed. I was now thinking perhaps it wasn't going to be so bad after all.

On Christmas Eve, about a dozen of us had a little party in our signals section. We had all managed to get plenty to eat, so really we didn't do at all badly. The party went off very well and afterwards we had a sing-song in the 9 Operations Room itself.

On Christmas morning, Henderson and I set off on a walk to our hilltop station, 12,000 feet up in the hills. When we got to the top, we had a cup of char and a chat with the lads. Then after wishing them all a Merry Christmas, set off back so we would be in time for dinner.

We had a swell Christmas dinner, with all one could wish for. All the officers helped us and made it as happy a time as possible. Afterwards, we managed to get some of the officers signatures, for keepsake, on the menu.

After we had a quiet lay down, we got washed and changed into our blue, for we needed it, and set off to the YMCA. Here we found a party in full swing. We started with a wizard tea of jellies, trifles and many other things. After tea, we all played party games then sang carols around the fire. I don't think enough praise could be given to these people for what they did for us. They were just wonderful. I know I was never able to thank them enough for what they did.

With Christmas over, we began to settle down to normal life again. Of course, we didn't mind, for we were still getting a very easy time.

It was on New Year's Day 1945 that Henderson and I set off to the hilltop station. All it consisted of was a transmitter remotely controlled from the valley below. All we had to do was just watch it and maintain it. We had a tent up there to live in and cooked all our own meals.

Each day we got fresh rations brought up from the valley by coolies and one BOR. Whenever he arrived, we always had a cup of char waiting for him and we would most likely play a game of cards before he went down.

Although we were only up there for ten days, they were the most pleasant days I had so far spent out here. We would rise about 8:00am and, going out of the tent, look down into the valley below. It was nearly always covered in mist at that time of the day, so all you could see was an occasional glance of the road. The two of us then cooked breakfast and settled down to a day spent lazing on top of the hill, sunbathing. In the evenings, we always went to bed early as there was little else to do. At night, whilst we lay in bed, we could hear the monkeys running up and down the tent, although we wondered whatever it was at first.

When we had been up there a few days, two nurses suddenly appeared from nowhere and we spent quite a pleasant hour speaking to them. Although they said they would be coming up again, they never did. On another day, we were visited by two flight lieutenants.

Soon after these two visits, we got orders to move and started dismantling our equipment. We soon got it all stripped down, although it took about 100 men to help carry it all down. We, of course, had our own kit so got off carrying any of the other stuff. The tent was left up there and for all I know is still there, if it has withstood the monsoon.

We were very sorry indeed to leave this place, but when I got down, I got a worse shock, for I was told three of us:

Johnny, a corporal and myself were off to a forward base in Burma in a few days time.

Two or three days of packing soon passed by and, before we knew where we were, it was Saturday 13th January, our day of departure.

We got up at 4:00am and after going along the icy bamboo path, we found the gharry awaiting us. Before we left, our Signals Officer cooked us our breakfast. We then set out for Tallihul, from where we were to fly to Burma.

CHAPTER IV

BURMA – THE LAND WE FOUGHT FOR

After many hours of hanging around, we eventually found ourselves airborne. We all sat watching the strip we had just left, slowly diminish into the distance. We were soon flying over thick jungle country and mountains, through which our 14th army had so gallantly fought. After about two hours flying, we crossed a large river which we presumed was the Chindwin.

Just after we had crossed this river, we heard a terrific bang on our port wing which made us all jump, for we thought perhaps a Jap had got us. A little later on, we landed on a strip which was still in the process of being built and which we soon found out was called Tabingon.

When we alighted from the 'kite,' we found out the cause of the bang in mid-air. It was where some big bird had hit us on our wing. I couldn't believe that a bird could make such a big dent as that.

Soon after we landed, we were sent to 906 Wing, where we were to work for a while. We were sent down to find a site for our VHF but, as usual with the RAF, we were caught in a totally different job, namely putting up and pulling down tents.

We had been there about four days, when the three of us were sent to Onbuck, a strip about four miles from the Japs' lines, where we were to set up some equipment.

It was from this strip that we watched our 'kites' bombing the Japs who were trying to cross the river. We were all very glad to get back from there to the camp. On the way back, our gharry broke down and, although we eventually did get it going, we did not get back until 9:00pm that night.

A few days later, our Signals Officer and Flight Sergeant arrived, so we were moved up to a site from which we were to operate the aircraft on the strip. Unlike Wing, where we had to work as soon as we arrived, we were first given tents and made comfortable. In fact we did not start work till the next morning.

Next day, we started to lay remote control lines and power lines prior to the transmitters and receivers arriving. Although it was very hard work setting all this equipment up, we enjoyed it very much, for when we had finished, everything was done for our comfort by our Signals Officer.

The camp itself was very nicely situated in a palm grove, so whenever we ate, our tent was always in the shade. In the evenings, we often went for a swim in a lovely canal which ran nearby. In the evenings we used to get all around the tents and have a lovely sing-song. Sometimes we were lucky enough to get a film show or even two.

After we had been there a fortnight, a day arrived which was tragic for us, for on this day our Signals Officer was accidentally shot. We were all very sorry about it, for he was such a great fellow and he had done everything possible for us. He was buried the next day with full military honours, just outside Shwebo. For a day or two after this, we were all very quiet indeed.

It was not many days afterwards that once more we were to dismantle the equipment so that we could move to a new strip nearer to Mandalay. We soon pulled everything down and were ready to move which, on February 2nd, we did. This time we were off for Sadaung, 30 miles north of Mandalay.

We left at about 7:00 am and were soon on the road to Shwebo. It did not take us very long to get there. Then we were on the 'Road to Mandalay,' although it was a lot different to the film version. About ten miles south of Shwebo, we stopped for a cup of char and something to eat. After we had finished we started up our gharry and, to our great dismay, it just stopped. After fiddling about with it for several hours, we eventually got it going and were once more on our way. When we eventually got to Sadaung - our new strip, our gharry broke down again, leaving us stranded just off the road.

That night we cooked our own food and settled down to bed. Whilst we lay in bed that night, we listened to the guns banging away just down the road. We didn't know if they were ours or the enemy's (or both). During that night we had a scare when we heard someone getting into our gharry but it was only our own guards.

The next day we were towed to the strip. It was still being built when we arrived and the army was in occupation of the place. We slept here for one night before being moved on to our final site where the equipment was to be set up.

At that time, we were eating and living with another MSU - that being number 5765. And since there were only three of us, we were very glad of this.

During our first few days here, we were issued with rum. In fact we needed it to keep our nerves steady, for we were in constant fear of Jap rear parties. All the same, nothing went wrong and we started to set up our equipment. On the second day of doing this, 9 Ops Room again arrived and after a few days of earnest work, we were once more set up and operational.

Sadaung was not as well situated as our last place for there was no cover from the burning sun, which was now beginning to get quite warm. Also, to make things worse there was an acute shortage of water so we were not so happy here.

When we got all the equipment going, we embarked onto a watch system again and were soon getting plenty of time off. We had only been there a few weeks when our Flight Sergeant decided to give us a board for our ACI so we all got down to some studying during the nights. One night brought us quite a scare when a Jap patrol was reported at the end of the strip. So down the trenches, which we had dug only a few days previously, we went, waiting for anything that may come. But, as luck would have it, nothing happened. We had to 'stand to' for the rest of the night but when morning came, we were given the all clear.

A few days later, we had our boards and all passed out with our ACI. And after a week of steady studying, we were very glad to have a rest from it. The day after our board, we saw Marie Burke in person. It was great to see her and made us forget where we were for quite a while.

About a week later, we went down to our corps camp, to see Francais Day in person, which again was to be a very good show. Even if we were in the forward areas, we were getting much more entertainment than we ever got in India.

We had been in Sadaung for about a fortnight when the boys arrived from Imphal, so once more we were all together. We were all glad to see them, for we knew once more we would be having fun again.

All the while up to now, we had been giving a lending hand to the 14th Army, giving them fighter cover to Mandalay. When Mandalay was finally captured on March 10th, we were just as excited as if we had captured it ourselves, instead of the small part we'd actually played. All the same, we were very proud of our role.

During the next few weeks, everything went along as normal. The only difference was the ever increasing heat, which was getting to around 100°F. In fact, by the last week in March, it finally beat me and I was taken to hospital with heat exhaustion. All the same, I very soon got over my attack and was back on the job.

When I came out of hospital they had started to dismantle the equipment, for once again we had orders to move.

A few days before we were due to leave, I met a fellow who came from Stretton, not five miles from home. We had an interesting chat which lasted till quite late at night. That night, we all slept in the open as we had all dismantled our tents. Of course, just out of spite, it had to pour with rain and there was one mad dash for the one tent which had been left up. Gosh what a panic!

On April 8th, we were once again on the move so, with 9 Operations Room, we set off for our new strip, which was across the Irrawaday. The journey as far as the river was uneventful. However, when we reached the river, we had to wait several hours to cross. So off we went on a scrounge for whatever we could find. And what we did find were lovely juicy melons, which we soon got our teeth into.

At about 3:00pm, we made our way down to the river where we were to cross. This place was called the Sagang

Bridgehead. Here we had to drive our gharries onto pontoons and were soon on our way over. These pontoons were made out of pontoon boats and sections of Bailey bridges. The whole set up, which carried three gharries, was pulled by a motor boat. Thank goodness we had air superiority, for we could have had a few bombs on us, being such a sitting target.

Once we reached the other side, we were off again, but we only travelled for about ten miles before we pulled into a field where we were staying the night. The first thing we did was to find a well where we could get a nice cold wash. This we soon found and were ready for dinner. That evening and night, we all took turns to do a guard, just in case anything unwanted turned up. We were all very glad when the next morning came and were once more on the road.

We travelled till about midday when we came to our new site and found all the aerials already up and ready for operations. Although, to the great disappointment of us, and those who put them up, they were to come down again to be put up in a different place.

Dwehlia, the place we were now at, was not too bad a place. It was again built in a palm grove and also partly in a deserted village. The best part was that there was a lovely river running nearby to it, where we could always go for a swim when off duty. The place had an everlasting smell of dead bodies, which we imagined were the Japs who had died fighting for it.

For the next ten days we were lucky to have very little work to do and spent most of our time swimming and taking everything at a leisurely pace.

One day, we even went off to Mandalay for a day. We left at about 9:00am, arriving there at midday. On the way to Mandalay, we saw the famous Ava Bridge, which still had its middle span missing - knocked out in our retreat in 1942. Of course, due to this, we had to cross by way of a pontoon bridge. When we arrived at Mandalay, our first object was to get a drink, which we got in a café.

There was actually very little left of Mandalay except for a few burnt out ruins. I don't think I saw a whole building standing in the town. All the same, it was nice to say you had visited Mandalay. On the way back, we took a good look at Pagoda Hill, where most of the fighting had been. It was a lovely sight to see all of the golden pagodas glistening in the sun. We passed through a village about ten miles outside where we were showered with fruits and flowers - gosh we felt like victors ourselves.

A few days after this trip, we were told we were going to Meiktila, where we were to pick up an armoured column and go right through enemy lines to set up our operations room.

This rumour was the start of many which were to follow.

CHAPTER V

THE DASH FOR RANGOON

The next day, on April 20th, we started a move which was to eventually land us at Mingaladon, just outside Rangoon. We set off in the morning fairly early and were soon speeding along a very nice road, just for a change. After travelling for a while, we came to the village of Kyauhse, or should I say, what was the ruins of it. For what was once a rich oil centre, now lay in a heap of burned out rubble. We had soon passed through and were out again on the main road. On we travelled till we came to the town of Meiktila, a scene of furious fighting not so long previously. Although the town had been fairly badly knocked about, there was still quite a lot left standing.

After leaving Meiktila behind, we soon left the main road and arrived at our new strip. Here, we once again found all of the equipment up, ready for operations. After a meal and putting up our tent, we soon got down to work. This time, we were to give a hand at Flying Central, which mainly meant checking lines and other odd jobs. It was on our second night there that we got quite a shock to find the Japs were mortaring the end of our strip. All the same, it did not last very long and we soon all got to bed.

This new strip was on a sandy plain with little sign of vegetation anywhere. The shortage of water supply was also acute, so we were all looking forward to getting out of the place - which we did do after a few days.

The next place we were going to was well over 100 miles away, so we knew we would have to travel for more than one day. We set off about 2:00pm and travelled till 6:00pm when we stopped for the night. We pulled in just off the road and parked all our gharries in box fashion, for we expected some trouble that night as the Japs were in the vicinity.

After a surprisingly quiet night, we set off early next morning. It was during this part of the journey that I saw many dead Japs, just left where they had fallen, which was not very pleasant, for our fellows had only passed by a few days earlier. I remember we often used to think during these journeys that if we weren't careful, we would be getting in front of our own men.

That evening when we arrived at the strip, called Souiss T, it was just getting dark. All our gharries had to go right round the strip to get to the site. Whilst we were waiting for the OK to go round the strip, it was lit up so some kites could take off. Jappy must have seen these, for about five minutes later, in he came with a lone kite and bombed and strafed the strip. Only one of the gharries got damaged, although three fellows were killed. This short but sharp raid certainly scared us for quite a while afterwards.

The following day, we set up our HF equipment so we could get further instructions from our base.

When we finally got through in the late afternoon, we were told to set up two channels of VHF. That night, several of us were put guarding the camp. It was a very eerie experience, for the moon shining made everything look so ghostly and we were all glad when the night was over.

The next day we set up the two channels but, as the army were moving so fast, we moved that afternoon. This time we were off to a place called Tenant, about 30 miles north of Taungoo. As it was a fairly short journey, we arrived there very soon.

Early next morning, we started setting up our equipment, which we got up in record time. In fact, we were operational by that afternoon. We only just got it up in time for, that night, it poured with rain. In fact, it continued to do so for the next few days.

All the while we had been on the road, we had very good food considering what the cooks were having to put up with. I don't think the food deteriorated all the while. In fact, in lots of ways it was steadily improving. It was some of the best food I had had for quite a long while.

We were supposed to have moved five days later but, due to the sudden change in the weather, we had to postpone it for several days. We did finally move on May 1st, setting off early in the morning, but we did not get very far, for at Taungoo we were held up for a whole day waiting to cross the river which was in flood.

It was about this time, I suffered a bout of dysentery, which I am glad to say soon passed off, for we were miles from any medical help.

The next day, when we finally did get across, we made quite good progress. Although, whilst we were crossing, we were being constantly shelled by the Japs from the overlooking hills.

That night, we fuelled up in some little town and slept.

After a fairly early start, we arrived at a place about 20 miles from Pegu, where we had to pull in to await instructions for our next move. Here, we learnt from some fellows that Rangoon was in our hands, so we were all very happy. It meant, all being well, we would be going there.

At this place, there was a little river running through the camp where we would swim and wash. It wasn't till a few days later that found out it was full of mines.

On May 8th, the war in Europe ended, so we had a little celebration. It wasn't much of V.E. night though as we were rationed to water. During the evening, we listened to Churchill's historic speech announcing the end of hostilities in Europe. Just at this moment, the clatter of machine gun fire broke the silence. The Japs had certainly chosen a nice place to counter attack. So, whilst the people back in Blighty were going mad with delight, we spent V.E. night in the ditches.

Two days later, we again moved to a 'drome 30 miles from Rangoon, called Zaciwyn. It was during this journey that a very curious thing happened. We came to a river, over which the bridge was down, so we had to cross by way of a railway bridge - a very strange experience. It was soon afterwards we arrived at our new station, about midday. And what a deadly place it looked.

There was nothing for miles except sandy desert, with little clumps of trees here and there. We were all soon down to work again and, once more, got our equipment up in record time. We had only been there a day when down came the rain again. It continued for day after day until finally we got a signal off, asking if we could change our site as we were being flooded out continually. As luck would have it, this was granted and we were moved to Mingaladon, a Royal Air Force peacetime camp.

Here we found things a lot different to what we had been used to for the last five months. First of all, being a peace time camp, we were in long brick billets, two storeys high. I, with all the rest of the lads, was upstairs where we had a very nice bedroom. There were only eight of us, all told, in the room, so we managed to keep it as clean and tidy as possible.

Of course, another reason why we were so happy with this place was that we were under dry cover and, with the monsoon now in full swing, we were glad of this. However, the food at this place deteriorated terribly to what we had been used to on the road down. To make it even worse, we were down to half rations, so you can well imagine us being fed up.

Once again, we set about getting our equipment on the air and we were soon back, once again, on the watch system. We used to take turns the same as Imphal except, being more experienced now, we only had one on at a time instead of two. We could have done with two there however, for we were continually having trouble with our power supplies, such as engines failing and standbys having to be started up.

About three weeks later, we heard that there was a pal of mine down at our new receiver site, so I set off not knowing who to expect. You can imagine my great surprise and joy when I found out it was Bob. So once again, after five months apart, Bob and I were together. It seemed too good to be true. Better still, two days later, we were moved down to Rangoon and were billeted right at the back of where he was.

We had been there a week, when I paid my first visit to Rangoon. We hitch hiked down, which took about an hour and a half. However, to our great disappointment, when we arrived there, we found far more damage than we had expected. In fact it was very quiet and sleepy. The smell, due to the sanitation still being out of order, made things worse. In fact, we were glad to get back to camp that afternoon.

As soon as I got down to Rangoon, I went sick for I had not been feeling too good of late. The medical officer said I was run down and was to take things easy for a few days, which I did.

Now we were in Rangoon, there were several cinema shows going and, as Bob was around, we often went to the pictures together or had a chat in each others' billet. Our billet was a two storey house with two rooms downstairs and four upstairs. Our little gang all slept in the one room downstairs where we had a fan, electric lights and also a shower. So we were quite well off in the new place and, once again, the food improved quite a lot.

After a few days, I started work again and was on wireless at our transmitter site, which meant looking after four sets of VHF. The site was in the middle of a common so there was plenty of interest there from people walking around and such like.

Perhaps now, I ought to say something about Rangoon. Although rather badly knocked about, they soon set about clearing things up. Before the war, I imagined it was quite a nice and modern city with modern conveyances such as trolley buses. The streets all ran parallel to each other so, from the air, it looked as if it was divided into small squares.

The main place of interest there was, of course, the famous Shwedagon, a lovely large pagoda temple. To get to the actual temple, you had to mount over 100 steps which were flanked by stalls selling thousands of different articles, especially Japanese occupation money. When you reached the top, you came across a large courtyard in which stood the Shwe Dragon, which was covered in gold leaf all over. All around its base stood thousands of little minarets and four main temples - one on each side.

In each temple was a Buddha, built of solid gold and studded with many different jewels. All the while you were in this temple, you were not allowed to wear shoes.

For the next few weeks, nothing of any importance happened, except that, once again, Bob was posted away, which came as quite a blow to me, for we had been having some good times, just of late.

About three days after Bob had gone, I went sick with pains in my right side and was soon put in 60 Mobile Field Hospital with acute appendicitis.

60 MFH was a large building divided into four wards. One, which was on the top floor, was for surgical, where all operations were carried out. Two were medical wards, for all categories not under operation heading. Of course, as usual, there had to be a special ward specifically for officers. Also, there were the sisters quarters and rooms for all other medical staff.

I was admitted at 12:00 and had had my operation by 3:00 that afternoon, although I didn't come round till 9:00pm. When I came round, I was given a sleeping draught by a sister and was soon asleep again. When I awoke next morning, I was surprised to find that, except for my side hurting, I had no other complaints.

The sister on duty washed me and brought me a cup of tea, which was my breakfast. For this first day, I was to have nothing to eat, but I survived! During the day, I had three visitors. One was a friend I had known at Imphal and who, like me, was in hospital. The other two were fellows off my unit.

In two or three days, I was eating normally and on the fourth day I was allowed up for a little while. At first, getting about was very difficult and I had to hobble around, taking a dozen or so steps before resting, and so on.

A week after the operation, the sister took out the stitches and I was able to get around much better.

Just a word of praise is needed here I think, for these sisters. They were doing some wonderful work for our lads who were in great pain and suffering.

A week later, I was told I was able to go on sick leave early the following week, so I went off to the billet to collect what things I would need and, also to get paid.

The following week, at 7:00 one morning, I left for Mingaladon airfield to begin my leave.

CHAPTER VI

Leave at Shillong Assam

As soon as we reached the airstrip, we got our breakfast and afterwards, were loaded into a Dakota. As we took off, it was pouring with rain, but when we had been airborne for some time, it cleared up and the sun came out once again. As I looked down at the fields below it all looked like one sheet of water, which had accumulated during the heavy monsoon rain.

We had been flying about five hours when we reached the coast and could see the airstrip on Chittagong Peninsular where we were to land.

After tiffin, we all boarded ambulances and were taken, not to the station as we should have been, but to the hospital by mistake! It was a large military hospital, totally different to the Royal Air Force one, for there was far too much discipline there.

After a couple of days there, I at last persuaded the powers that be that I was going on leave, so they let me go to the station where I got onto the Sylhet train. I was very glad when the train finally pulled out and on its way. We travelled all night and arrived at a small station fifty miles from Sylhet where we had to change trains.

At about 2:00pm that afternoon, we got our train and were soon winding our way up through the hills in which Sylhet stood. During the afternoon, we passed through areas of flooded paddy fields. It was funny to see boats moving from field to field.

At 6:00pm, we arrived at Sylhet and were transported to the transit camp where we were to sleep that night. We were back on the road again early the next morning. We started climbing as soon as we left and were very quickly up in the hills. We slowly climbed until we were at 3,000 feet where we had to wait for an hour till the one way gate opened for us. When we did get through the gate, we started twisting and turning our way through the hills, up and up until we reached 10,000 feet. In doing so, we had passed through some very lovely country, including rushing torrents and waterfalls, deep ravines and steep sided cliffs.

When we reached the top, we stopped at a WVS hostel, where we had a decent feed and soon afterwards, finished the journey.

We arrived at Shillong at about 4:00pm and went up to the reception camp. Here, we were issued with more blankets as we were told it got very cold at night.

Next morning, we went before a medical officer who gave us our sick leave. I got only a fortnight, which was a bit of a disappointment - I expected at least three weeks. So, after the usual preliminaries, we were told we were now free.

Shillong is a fairly large town which lies up in the Khasi Hills. Of course, being in the hills makes it very straggly, with all of its streets going up or down. As it was a health resort, there were quite a few Europeans there, who were either tea planters or officers' wives. I myself found it one of the nicest towns in India.

There were many lovely walks up there, which took us over hills, by waterfalls and many other glorious sights. The climate up there being lovely and cool made it possible for one to play all sorts of sports, although during my time there I had the misfortune to visit during the rainy season.

The fortnight spent up there quickly went by and I was soon on my last night.

Next morning, we started the long descent down to the Brahmaputra, which I was once again to cross, this time going westwards. The road down to the village was more or less like the one coming up except it went straight down. After twisting and turning for four hours, we reached the river where we got a very welcome meal.

We crossed the river early in the afternoon and were soon on our way to Calcutta. The journey was uneventful except for the excitement prevailing due to the startling news of Japan asking for surrender terms.

When we arrived at Calcutta the next morning, there was no fresh news of the war situation so we were disappointed. We firstly made our way to the transit camp where we were given our sleeping quarters. Then, after a decent wash, we set off to see Calcutta - a different Calcutta to the one we'd seen last time, for now there was no black out.

Chowringhee, Calcutta's Oxford Street, was just one blaze of light from shop windows and cinemas. It was a glorious sight, I think the best lit since Bombay.

We had only been in Calcutta a few days when the Japanese decided to surrender. This came as great news for it meant a much earlier homecoming, or so we hoped.

Calcutta did its best to celebrate by floodlighting the whole city. All the government buildings and places of importance were floodlit by many different coloured lights, making everything look very impressive indeed. Also, Firpas did their bit by opening their doors and giving all the forces a free meal.

So that was V.J. night in Calcutta, nothing as impressive as in Blighty, but all the same, much more exciting than V.E. night in Burma.

A few days later, Ron, a fellow I was knocking about with, introduced me to a civilian friend of his, who invited us both to dine that night. This was the first time I had ever been invited out so I was greatly looking forward to it. First we had soup, followed by chicken with all the accessories, finishing up with ice cream and, of course, coffee.

After this lovely food, we had a quiet chat around the table and prepared to leave. To my great delight, he asked if we could come to tea the following Sunday. Of course, our reply was yes! On the Sunday, we went to tea after having a very welcome bath. After tea, we went to chapel then came back to dinner. Gosh, were we leading lives of "Burah Sahilis," we certainly were.

For the three weeks to follow, we were often to visit our friend and dine with him. After being in Calcutta a month, we were told there was a boat waiting to take us to Rangoon, so our life of ease was finishing. We said goodbye to our friend, thanking him for all he had done for us to make our stay so happy. This was just another of the few cases of kindness we met out there and were very grateful for.

The next morning, we all got aboard the boat. She was a small cattle ship, that was to take us all to Rangoon. Many of the fellows on board her were going there for the first time, so most of us shot a terrible line about how grim it was down there. This, of course, was the usual procedure in the forces.

The first day, we spent sailing down the River Hooghly, on which Calcutta stands, about 150 miles inland.

It was a fairly interesting journey, for we had many places to see on the way down to the open sea.

As usual, as we had seen all the way through India, we saw a great deal of poverty. Towards evening, we saw the land slowly vanishing on either side and we were soon in open sea.

We were at sea for three days, during which we had a very easy time indeed, doing very little work. On the fourth morning, we entered the Rangoon River, on which the town of the same name lies. We twisted and turned up the river till we reached our anchoring place at about 9:00am.

We were all loaded into gharries and taken to a transit camp and on to our respective units. As I had just come off leave, I went back to 9 Ops Room, which I soon found out was now 6 Ops Room, as it had changed during my absence. So once more I was back at work, although not for long as I was soon to find out.

CHAPTER VII

LEAVING RANGOON

The first thing I did when getting back off leave was, of course, check to see how much mail there was for me. I was very pleased to find about 50 letters so, that evening, I promptly got down to answering a few of them. It was whilst I was doing this that a funny coincidence occurred. I had just started to answer Bob's letter, which was the oldest, when a voice behind me said, "I shouldn't bother to answer that," and who should it be but Bob.

Funnily enough, he had only been in Rangoon just over a couple of days, so once again we were reunited for the first time in just over a month.

The first few hours we spent together, we spoke mainly of where we had been and what we had done since our last meeting. We then went round to the Nuffield Club and had a meal and continental with our chat. The Nuffield club was opened for the Royal Air Force in Rangoon. It was a very nice place, having every form of entertainment possible. The club helped us to pass away many happy hours during the remaining time of our stay in Rangoon.

As soon as I came back, I was put to work on our receiver site for a change. It was quite nice there and not quite so lonely as at transmitters. I was once more put on a watch system and soon fell into a lazy life again, with little work and plenty of pleasure.

We spent quite a bit of our time at Victoria Lakes, which were a few miles outside the city. Here, there was The Boat Club, which had a cinema, canteen and rubber dinghies for rowing in. I and my friend spent many hours rowing and sunbathing on these lovely natural lakes.

During the evening, Bob and I either went to the pictures or played a few games of chess. We always managed to pass the evenings away very quickly. So, of course, when it came time for Bob to go again, it became very hard. But, as we were soon to move again, I didn't mind so much. Bob meanwhile, went up to Bangkok in Thailand.

The day after Bob departed, our unit left 6 Ops Room for good and joined the much larger Mobile Signals Unit 5771. With this unit, we were supposed to have gone to Sumatra, but as we were later to find out, this wasn't to be the case.

When we got round to the new billet, which was only in the next road, we were shown around and had the rest of the day off to settle in. In fact, except for the first three days there, when we saw that all our equipment was serviceable, we spent the next three weeks at leisure.

We spent most of our time playing tennis, badminton or walking. In the evening, it was a case of either go to the pictures or stay in. On this unit, being a much smaller one, we found the fellows much more friendly and willing to give a lending hand.

At the beginning of the third week there, we started on driving instruction but, due to our posting coming through suddenly, we had to give it up. We were off the Sumatra draft and were going with another unit to Penang!

About 6:00 on the evening of 1st November, we set off to find the dock where we were to board ship. As usual, it had been left too late to set off and we had to spend the night on a piece of derelict land, sleeping on top of the gharries. Stan, Johnny and I slept on top of one gharry and had just got off to sleep, when a thunderstorm broke. Gosh, did we get wet.

Next morning, we drove into the dockyard and were told we couldn't be loaded for three days. This meant, either taking the gharries back to the unit or two of us staying behind to guard them. The latter was chosen and Johnny and I stayed behind.

We enjoyed this stay for we had nothing to do but watch the gharries by day and, at night, we moved off up town to the pictures or something.

On the third day, we all got aboard the boat, which was called SS Carlton. It was quite a pleasant ship. The next morning we were called very early and watched them load our gharries on board, which we were glad to see for it meant goodbye to Rangoon, which we weren't sorry to say.

All the gharries were on by 9:00am and, by full tide at 11:00, we were slowly moving down the River Rangoon, the river I had come up three months previously.

As we sailed on during the afternoon, we took our last look at Burma, the last I hoped I would ever see of it. And, as dusk began to fall, we saw the Burmese coast slowly diminishing on both sides of us.

SS Carlton was a 12,000 ton ship used for carrying heavy cargoes. All of the holds were loaded with our gharries, except the one we were loaded into.

All the food, we cooked ourselves, which turned out surprisingly well. All of the crew of the ship were friendly with us and let us see most parts of the ship.

During our first day at sea, like most days at sea, there was nothing to see but water. I sat right at the very front of the ship sunbathing most of the time and looking around for anything of interest. It was a glorious day and although the boat was going steadily south, it got no hotter.

The second and third days were more or less the same as the first except in the evening of the third day, we saw a curious sight. Right in front of the boat, there were about half a dozen porpoises dodging and zigzagging in front of the ship. It was a marvellous sight to see the ship gaining on them until, when it caught up with them, they just sheared off.

The final day we awoke to a wet and dismal morning making it very cool on board. Later on in the afternoon, the sun came out and we saw the coast of Malaya for the first time. As we slowly drew closer, we could see nothing but swamp. At about 4:00pm, we started to make our way up a lagoon in which Port Swettenham stood. On either side of the lagoon there was typical palm country. We were soon anchored in the bay, waiting to be taken off once the ship in front had unloaded.

Early next morning, we started unloading but, as our gharry was one of the first on, it was one of the last off. By mid afternoon, we were taken off the boat by a launch first, leaving three drivers for the gharries.

We had now landed in the third country of my tour since leaving Blighty - Malaya.

CHAPTER VIII

MALAYA AND ITS CONTRASTS

It was 12th November when we first set foot on Malayan soil at Port Swettenham, a fair sized port about 200 miles north of Singapore. As soon as we were on dry land, we set out to do a little bit of exploring and getting a first hand impression of Malaya. This was rather difficult with it being nearly dark when we landed. However, we soon found out we could get iced drinks and something to eat at the railway station.

After hanging around for a few hours, we got our gharries off and set off for a billet where we were to sleep before moving on, the following morning, to Kuala Lumpur the capital of Malaya some 40 miles away.

When we got to the billet, we were surprised to see Chinese girls everywhere. When we asked who they were, we found out they did all of the laundry and kept the billets clean. As soon as we got in the billet, they were all around us, wanting to make our beds and do odd jobs for us.

The next morning, we left at about 10:00am and were soon travelling along the road. We could now get a much better impression of Malaya. The roads were perfect in comparison with Burmese roads. They rolled along very strangely, in between groves of rubber trees, some of which were being tapped for sap. All along the roads, the children cheered us, just as if we were the liberators.

The people were also very much more friendly and healthy looking. The fairer sex seemed to dress much more like Europeans and seemed more attractive than we had seen in other eastern countries. Of course, here we came across several nationalities.

Firstly, there were the Malayans, who were the true inhabitants of the country. They are mostly dark skinned, not quite as dark as in India and all fairly short. They seem to be a hard working people and rather shy in lots of ways.

The second most populous group in the country are the Chinese, who are unlike most eastern nationalities, very light skinned. Some of the women are very beautiful in their ways. These people, except for the coolie class, seem to run most of the business concerns in Malaya.

The other two classes are the Indians and Eurasians. Many of the Eurasians are fairly important people. They nearly all wear European dress.

We arrived at Kuala Lumpur, the new capital of Malaya, about midday and were very much impressed by the modernness of the city. There were large municipal buildings built in very modern style. The government buildings were built to an eastern pattern with minarets and domes, making them very beautiful indeed. The streets were wide with modern shops all the way along - quite a contrast to what we had seen in Burma.

After passing right through the town, we came to the camp where we were to stay for a day or two whilst all our gharries were seen to. As it turned out, we stayed for a week in the end, which just gave us time to see the place properly.

As soon as it was evening, and we could get out, we set off for a tour of the place. Our first stop was at the NAAFI, where we could get a good feed and all the "gen" on it. After we left the NAAFI, we took a fi-rickshaw to the first place of amusement. Perhaps I should explain what a fi-rickshaw is. It is a bicycle with a small side carriage, capable of carrying two, attached to the side of it. They were surprisingly quick things to get about in, especially when going downhill, where one often reached a speed of 20mph or more.

The first place we came to was an amusement park, where there was plenty to do to pass the time away. After amusing ourselves for an hour or so, we went dancing. Gosh, wasn't it funny to see dozens of girls to dance with. In fact, instead of four girls to every 100 fellows, as in Burma, it was more like the opposite here.

As the evening went very quickly, it was soon midnight so we made off for the billet.

On the following day, we went to a cinema where it seemed so marvellous, after being used to wooden forms and no fans, sitting in plush seats with fans going all the while. It also seemed very queer having a girl usherette to show you to your seat.

During the rest of the week, we either went sight seeing or to some amusement park. Anyway, it was just like a holiday and cheap, for the prices were very low.

We were all very sorry when the day came for us to leave, for we had had a grand time there. We set off about 7:00am and were soon rolling across open country along a very good road. Before we came to our next large town of Ipoh, we had to cross a large range of mountains, about 6,000ft. It was a glorious ride climbing then dropping all the way along for many miles. As we slowly drew nearer to Ipoh, we saw signs of her great industry - tin! There were many mines where one could see the damage done by the Japs.

Ipoh itself was very much smaller than Kuala Lumpur. We only stayed just the one night and, except for a few glimpses of some of the municipal buildings, we saw very little else.

The next morning, we were on the road early and were once more passing through very lovely country, which could easily be mistaken for English countryside. Once again, we had to pass through mountains to get to the other side where Butterworth, the terminus of the road to Penang lay.

We arrived there at midday and soon found an empty house for a billet before moving over to the island itself. We only stopped in Butterworth for one night, although we were to return over a week later.

The following morning, we awoke early and were on the ferry by midday.

When we reached the island, we went up to camp, which was a few miles out of Georgetown, the capital of Penang Island. It was a peacetime camp, built on a hill overlooking the straits. It was a glorious view there, for in front of us was the sea and behind us, the hills rising to 2,000ft.

Georgetown itself, which we saw that evening, was a large modern town with many three storey buildings. There were wide streets and all modern conveniences. There were also four modern cinemas of air conditioned type.

In contrast to all places we had been to before, we found many cafes and other places of amusement, as well as pictures. There were two amusement parks and also two dance halls. The main dance hall, called "City Lights," was a fair sized place with 100 to 150 girls acting as hostesses. As we came to find out very soon, dancing was very expensive - an entry fee of 60 cents, followed by 25 cents for each dance, which soon mounted up if you had a lot of dances.

After we had been on the island for a week, we were moved back again to the mainland, to Butterworth Airstrip, which was about three miles outside the village itself.

The camp was very nicely situated in a palm tree grove, less than 100 yards from the sandy beach and the Straits of Malacca. Of course, being situated so near to the coast, it had a lovely cool breeze flowing through it most of the time.

When we reached the camp, we were put into tents as there was no room in the billets. As usual, we were four to a tent and soon settled down to the old routine again.

When we reported to our signals section a few days later, we were set to work on building a receiver site. Quite a lot of time was devoted to chopping down palm trees which were causing excessive screening to our aerials. After we had cleared up the site and got it into a more or less decent working state, we settled down to getting our VHF equipment ready for setting up our transmitter site.

Whilst we were doing this, the time passed quickly and we were soon drawing near to Christmas. It was a week before this that I had a board for my LAC and passed it.

Christmas 1945 arrived and we all set out to have as good a time as possible. On Christmas Eve, Joe and I went into town to the Piccadilly, our favourite hotel, where we listened to the band playing Christmas music and danced with a few of the waitresses there, who were all Eurasians. We saw Christmas Day in, then caught the last ferry back to camp.

When Christmas morning dawned, after the usual 'Merry Christmas,' we got up to a wizard breakfast consisting of: grapefruit, eggs and bacon and bread, butter and marmalade. After breakfast had settled itself down, we went for a long walk along the beach.

When dinner came around, we all made our way to the cookhouse and seated ourselves at the table awaiting the officers and sergeants to look after us. We had soup, chicken or duck and its usual accessories, followed by Christmas pudding with brandy sauce. After spending the rest of the afternoon sleeping it off, we had a little tea and were once more off to Penang.

Again, we went to the Piccadilly, where we had a little party for four of us and four waitresses. Although there was no spirit as we would have found at home, we had a reasonably good time and it was 2:00 before we turned into bed at the hotel.

On Boxing Day, when we got downstairs, we found ourselves in the midst of a wedding breakfast, to which we were immediately invited. After the party, at which everyone spoke English and acted as if they were our fellow countrymen, we set off for a walk around town.

In the afternoon, we found ourselves getting a little bit bored, so we set off back to camp. When we got back, we had a wash and tidy up and, after dinner, went to the station dance.

However, Joe and I, who didn't dance, soon decided to take a trip over to the island again, where we bought some fire crackers and started chucking them all around

Penang. The evening passed by very quickly and it was soon midnight and Christmas was over. It was time for us to settle down again and, by the time the new year came in, we were once again back in the old quiet routine.

1946 started well with a glorious hot day during which we spent most of the time on the nearby beach. The first month of the year saw nothing much exceptional, except for the opening of our new transmitter site, which was opened up during the first week. Also worth mentioning was my promotion to LAC during the same month.

We spent most of our off time now either sunbathing, swimming or occasionally going down town. Life was really quiet until the second week of February when an ammunition dump blew up on the airstrip!

My first indication of the incident was a terrific bang, followed by a blast, blowing through the tent. Bombs and torpedoes were going off all day at infrequent intervals. Of course, the airstrip was out of commission for quite a while until it was all made safe once more.

It wasn't until the last few days of March that any event worth mentioning occurred. On this day we were moved to our new camp, three miles nearer to Butterworth. This time, we were all put into bashas instead of tents, which were very much more comfortable, although with no privacy. The camp was built in a proper military style, in barrack blocks, but we were soon used to it, preferring it to our previous camp.

Once again, we were soon put to work at our new transmitter site, where we had quite a few more channels than previously at 60 staging post. It was very well laid out and the working conditions were much better than previously. All of the equipment was now in gharries instead of tents, making everything much more waterproof.

We soon got ourselves settled down to this new life and, before we knew where we were, Easter had arrived. Work still had to continue through Easter, although we were lucky to get Saturday off, which was also V Day. A few of us spent a very pleasant afternoon swimming off the island. In the evening, we had a good meal and watched the Chinese procession, which seemed to consist more of flags than anything else. Anyway, it turned out to be a most enjoyable day and we were all very tired when we got back to the billet.

During the next few months, fellows who were our pals, were all going home on demobilisation, so we were constantly having parties and farewells. We were very sorry to be parted, but I expect the fellows were all glad to be heading homewards.

During the last few weeks of our second year overseas, we had a short week leave. Johnny and I spent a glorious week at Fort Auchry. It was a camp built on the cliffs about 10 miles outside Georgetown. It had its own private beach, where we used to lie each day, sunbathing or swimming. In the evenings, we went into town to a dance or to the pictures.

One day, we went to the top of Penang Hill, which was very interesting, especially the journey up by the mountain railway. Another place we visited was a private swimming pool, built inside a house owned by a rich Chinese banker. We were both sorry when it had finished and we had to go back to camp.

The rest of my second year overseas saw me remain at Butterworth, without incident.

It was during the last week in August that my posting came through, this time to the Middle East. I took rather a poor view to this posting as I had already served two years in this command and I didn't see why I should have my tour messed up by moving such a long distance. Of course, there it was and what the RAF say, went!

Anyway, this posting didn't last long for, on the morning of 28th August, I was told I was going home on release! Imagine my joy and happiness at even the thought of going home. It was all too good to be true.

After that, it was just one mad panic to get cleared release medicals, clearance chits and all those sort of things.

Anyhow, I was soon done and, by that evening, was on the first leg of my journey home!

CHAPTER IX

GOING HOME AT LAST!

I left Butterworth at 7:00 that Wednesday night for Pria, from where I was to catch the train to Singapore. It was quite dark when we left Pria. We then travelled all night, arriving at Kuala Lumpur early next morning. We then had to wait until 6:00 that evening for a connection so I spent the day in the NAAFI, watching my kit and having a good feed.

We left at 6:00, once again travelling all night. At about 8:00 the next morning, as typical of Malayan trains, the engine broke down, so we had to wait for three hours whilst they fetched a replacement from Johore Causeway.

Whilst we were waiting there, we saw the Sultan's palace, which looked very eastern, as one would imagine it.

The causeway was disappointing, being of brick construction and joining the island to Johore town. Once we were on the island, we soon reached Singapore.

When we finally arrived at Singapore station, 14 hours late, we had to wait another 3 hours for transport to the transit camp situated at Jengal, 16 miles outside of

Singapore. Here I was messed about, not knowing if I was coming or going. One moment I was going home by air, the next by sea. It finally turned out to be by sea, leaving for the dock at 6:00 on the morning of 15th September.

It was a very cold journey that morning, coming down through the mist to the docks. As we got there, we quickly boarded SS Britannic, which was to have sailed that afternoon. There were quite a few people to see us off including a military band. But due to a last minute hitch, we didn't leave till next morning.

As I watched the docks of Singapore slowly disappear, it was a wonderful feeling at last to be going home!

We slowly wended our way through the hundreds of tiny islets along the coast of Singapore and the Straits settlement of Johore. Seeing them from the boat, they all looked beautiful and just as they should have looked, giving one rather the wrong impression of them.

We travelled up and along the coast of Malaya, following it fairly closely. About tea time on our first day of sailing, we passed Port Swettenham, where I had landed 10 months previously. On we travelled all day and by sunset were still in sight of land.

The next day, the 18th, we saw land on our port bow, which we soon found out was Sumatra. By that evening, we had passed around its northern tip and into the Indian Ocean.

The journey across the Indian Ocean took two days and, by the evening of the 20th, we had passed Ceylon, not that we saw it, for it was late at night. It was a very pleasant journey, with calm seas and a fresh breeze, enabling us to get plenty of sunbathing in.

The following day, we saw the Isle of Minicoy, which was used as a refuelling base for our ships during the war.

By the 24th, we saw the Isle of Socotra, which stands in the entrance to the Gulf of Aden. We passed Aden at 2:00am on the 26th, so didn't see it. During the day however, we saw many islands including the Twelve Apostles which are twelve barren rocks sticking out from the sea.

We arrived at Port Suez early on the morning of the 29th, dropping anchor for about two hours. We entered the canal at about 9:00am, going past the memorial commemorating the troops whose lives were lost in its defence.

For the first 20 miles we passed through nothing but sand, then continued through the two great lakes. We then came to the first of many rest centres where British troops, both male and female, spent their leave. The canal itself, which we had previously travelled down, still proved very interesting to us all, especially as we had a laugh at the troops on the coast, for this time we were going the right way.

The last few hours of the journey were done in darkness, with the aid of a massive searchlight at the front of the boat.

We arrived at Port Said at 9:00 and spent most of the night bargaining with the Arabs over goods. I managed to buy some fruit at least.

Next morning, when I awoke, we were already moving and all I saw of Port Said was the town vanishing behind us.

We sailed on all through that day and the next and it wasn't until 4:00 on the afternoon of the 2nd that we saw, from a distance, the British George Cross island of Malta.

The next morning, we saw the coast of Africa, which we followed for the rest of the day, passing Algeria and its capital, Algiers, in the evening.

After that, we saw no land until we passed Gibraltar at 10:00 on the night of the 4th. We saw very little of it, which was rather disappointing.

We were now on the final stage of our journey, having passed into the Atlantic Ocean.

We passed Cape St Vincent, the southernmost tip of Portugal, at 10:00am on October 5th. The sea was still very calm and, although it was rather cold, it was quite pleasant weather.

The next day, we crossed the Bay of Biscay with no incidents, for the sea remained moderately calm.

It wasn't until 8:00am on the 7th that we saw England!

It was the northern coast of the mouth of the Mersey. Gosh, what a marvellous feeling it was to see England once again.

We docked at 10:00 where there was quite a crowd of people to meet us. It was surprising how far some people must have travelled to meet their loved ones, who they no doubt hadn't seen for years.

Well, this is about where the story of my tour overseas ends and, although I was glad to see England again, and although I was often fed up with my tour, I really wouldn't have missed any part of it for the whole world. It was all so very interesting and instructive and well worth the while.

In fact, I saw what lots of people would have paid thousands to see in peace time.

THE END

COUNTRY	TOWN/SITE	DATE ARR	DATE DEP	UNIT
England	Home	—	14-4-43	Join Up
	Padgate	14-4-43	21-4-43	3 receiving U
	Blackpool	21-4-43	12-5-43	5 Radio Sc
	Padgate	12-5-43	4-8-43	3 receiving U
	Home	4-8-43	11-8-43	Leave
	Padgate	11-8-43	13-8-43	3 receiving U
	Eltham	13-8-43	4-11-43	5 Radio Sc
	Home	4-11-43	13-11-43	Leave
	Eltham	13-11-43	3-3-44	5 Radio Sc
	Home	3-3-44	10-3-44	Leave
	Bolton	10-3-44	2-7-44	6 Radio Sc
	Home	2-7-44	16-7-44	Leave
	Blackpool	16-7-44	20-8-44	On draft
	Glasgow	20-8-44	21-8-44	On draft
India	Bombay	22-9-44	2-10-44	On draft
	Sambre	3-10-44	16-11-44	7 B Sig U
	Calcutta	20-11-44	28-11-44	Transit
	Imphal	2-12-44	13-1-45	
Burma	Tabingon	13-1-45	21-1-45	5837 MSU ATT 9 Ops
	Sadaung	21-1-45	8-4-45	
	Mandalay	9-4-45	20-4-45	
	Quentia	20-4-45	23-4-45	
	Tenant	24-4-45	5-5-45	
Burma	Pegu	7-5-45	10-5-45	5837 MSU ATT 9 Ops
	Zaquin	10-5-45	17-5-45	
	Mingaladon	17-5-45	23-7-45	
	Rangoon	23-6-45	23-7-45	

COUNTRY	TOWN/SITE	DATE ARR	DATE DEP	UNIT
India	Shillong	23-7-45	12-8-45	Sick Leave
	Calcutta	13-8-45	10-9-45	
Burma	Rangoon	15-9-45	7-11-45	5837 MSU
Malaya	Port Swettenham	12-11-45	13-11-45	Transit
	Kuala Lumpur	13-11-45	17-11-45	
	Ipoh	17-11-45	18-11-45	
	Penang	19-11-45	28-11-45	5837 ATT181 W
	Butterworth	28-11-45	30-8-46	
	Singapore	1-9-46	16-9-46	Transit
England	Liverpool	7-10-46	7-10-46	
	Marton	7-10-46	9-10-46	Demobbing
	Home	9-10-46	—	Demobbed

B Sig U: Base Signals Unit
MSU: Mobile Signals Unit
Ops: Operations Room
W: Wing